ORGANIZATION, OBJECTS,

AND

PLAN OF OPERATIONS,

OF THE

Emigrant Aid Company:

ALSO

A DESCRIPTION OF KANSAS.

FOR THE INFORMATION OF EMIGRANTS.

BOSTON:
PRINTED BY ALFRED MUDGE & SON,
No. 21 School Street.
1854.

Secretary's Office.—At the Massachusetts Historical Society's Rooms, over the Institution for Savings, next door south of the Museum, Tremont Street, Boston.

EMIGRANT AID COMPANY.

For the purpose of answering numerous inquiries, concerning the plan of operation of the Emigrant Aid Company, and the resources of Kansas Territory, which it is proposed now to settle, the Secretary of the Company has deemed it expedient to publish the following definite information in regard to these particulars:

I. THE COMPANY'S OBJECTS AND PLANS.

The objects of this Association are apparent in its name.

The immense emigration to America from Europe introduces into our ports a very large number of persons eager to pass westward. The fertility of our western regions, and the cheapness of the public lands, induce many of the native born citizens of the old States also to emigrate thither. At the present time public and social considerations of the gravest character render it desirable to settle the territories west of Missouri and Iowa; and these considerations are largely increasing the amount of westward emigration.

The foreign arrivals in America, last year, were 400,777. In the same year, the emigration to Western States, of Americans and foreigners, must have amounted to much more than 200,000 persons. The emigration thither, this year, will be larger still. And from the older Western States large numbers are removing into new territory.

Persons who are familiar with the course of movement of this large annual throng of emigrants, know that under the arrangements now existing they suffer at every turn. The frauds practised upon them by "runners" and other agents of transporting lines in the State of New York, amount to a stupendous system of knavery: which has not been broken up even by the patient endeavors of the State officers, and by very stringent State legislation. The complete ignorance as to our customs in which the foreign emigrant finds himself, and in more than half the foreign emigration, his complete ignorance of our language, subjects him to every fraud, and to constant accident. It is in the face of every conceivable inconvenience, that the Country receives every year four hundred thousand foreigners into its seaports, and sends the larger portion of them to its Western Country.

The inconveniences and dangers to health to which the pioneer is subject who goes out alone or with his family, only in making a new settlement, are familiar to every American.

The Emigrant Aid Company has been formed to PROTECT EMIGRANTS, as far as may be, from such inconveniences. Its duty is to *organize emigration to the West and bring it into a system.* This duty, which should have been attempted long ago, is particularly essential now, in the critical position of the western territories.

It has been decided to execute a deed of trust in lieu of the charter granted by the Legislature, and it is believed that by an immediate subscription to this fund of two hundred thousand dollars the emigrant may be protected: a free State may be secured to the lasting advantage of the Country; and possibly a valuable property secured to the subscribers.

The emigrant suffers whenever he goes alone into his new home. He suffers from the frauds of others—from his own ignorance of the system of travel; and of the country where he settles; and, again, from his want of support from neighbors—which results in the impossibility of any combined assistance, or of any division of labor.

The Emigrant Aid Company will relieve him from all these embarrassments, by sending out emigrants in companies, and establishing them in considerable numbers. They will locate these where they please on arrival in their new home, and receive from government their titles. The Company propose to carry them to their homes more cheaply than they could otherwise go—to enable them to establish themselves with the least inconvenience, and to provide the most important prime necessities of a new colony. It will provide shelter and food at the lowest prices after the arrival of emigrants, while they make the arrangements necessary for their new homes. It will render all the assistance which the information of its agents can give. And, by establishing emigrants in large numbers in the territories, it will give them the power of using at once those social influences which radiate from the church, the school, and the press, in the organization and development of a community.

For these purposes, it is recommended, 1st, that the Trustees contract immediately with some one of the competing lines of travel for the conveyance of 20,000 persons from Massachusetts, to that place in the West which the Trustees shall select for their first settlement.

It is believed that passage may be obtained, in so large a contract, at a much less price than that paid by individuals. We recommend that emigrants receive the full advantage of this diminution of price, and that they be forwarded in companies of two hundred, as they apply, at these reduced rates of travel.

2nd. It is recommended that at such points as the Trustees select for places of settlement, they shall at once construct a boarding house or receiving house—in which three hundred persons may receive temporary accommodation on their arrival, and that the number of such houses be enlarged as necessity may dictate. The new comers or their families may thus be provided for, in the necessary interval which elapses while they are making their selection of a location.

3d. It is recommended that the Trustees procure and send forward steam saw mills, grist mills, and such other machines as shall be of constant service in a new settlement,—which cannot however be purchased or carried out conveniently by individual settlers. These machines may be leased or run by the Company's agents. At the same time, it is desirable that a printing press be sent out, and a weekly newspaper established. This would be the organ of the Company's agents:—would extend information regarding its settlement, and be from the very first, an index of that love of freedom and of good morals, which it is to be hoped may characterize the State now to be formed.

4th. It is recommended that the Company's agents locate, and take up for the Company's benefit the sections of land in which the boarding houses and mills are located,—and no others. And further, that whenever the territory shall be organized as a free State, the Trustees shall dispose of all its interests there, replace by the sales the money laid out, declare a dividend to the Stockholders;—and

5th. That they then select a new field, and make similar arrangements for the settlement and organization of another free State of this Union.

With the advantages attained by such a system of effort, the Territory selected as the scene of operations, would, it is believed, at once fill up with free inhabitants. There is reason to suppose that several thousand men of New England origin, propose to emigrate under the auspices of some such arrangement this very summer. Of the whole emigration from Europe,—amounting to some 400,000 persons, there can be no difficulty in inducing thirty or forty thousand to take the same direction. Applications from German agents have already been made to members of the Company, We have also intimations in correspondence from the free States of the West, of a wide spread desire there among those who know what it is to settle a new country to pass on, if such an organization can be made into that now thrown open. An emigrant party of those intending to go has been formed in Worcester County, and others in other States.

In view of the establishment by such agencies of a new Free State in that magnificent region, it is unnecessary to dwell in detail on the advantages which this enterprise holds out to the Country at large.

It determines in the right way the institutions of the unsettled Territories, in less time than the discussion of them has required in Congress. It opens to those who are in want in the Eastern States, a home and a competence, without the suffering hitherto incident to emigration. For the Company is the pioneer,—and provides, before the settler arrives, the conveniences which he first requires. Such a removal of an overcrowded population, is one of the greatest advantages to Eastern cities. *Again, the enterprise opens commercial advantages to the commercial States, just in proportion to the population which it creates, of free men who furnish a market to our manufactures and imports. Whether the new line of States shall be Free States or Slave States, is a question deeply interesting to those who are to provide the manufactures for their consumption. Especially will it prove an advantage to Massachusetts, if she create the new State by her foresight—supply the first necessities to its inhabitants—and open, in the outset, communications between their homes and her ports and factories.*

In return for these advantages, which the Company's rapid and simple effort affords to the emigrant and to the country, its Stockholders receive that satisfaction, ranked by Lord Bacon among the very highest, of becoming founders of States,* and

* See Mr. Everett's Speech on the Nebraska Bill.

more than this,—States which are prosperous and free. They secure satisfaction by an investment which promises large returns at no distant day.

Under the plan proposed, it will be but two or three years before the Company can dispose of its property in the Territory first occupied—and reimburse itself for its first expenses. At that time,—in a State of 70,000 inhabitants, it will possess several reservations of 640 acres each,—on which its boarding houses and mills stand,—and the churches and school houses which it has rendered necessary. From these centres will the settlements of the State have radiated. In other words, these points will then be the large commercial positions of the new State. If there were only one such,—its value, after the region should be so far peopled, would make a very large dividend to the Company which sold it, besides restoring its original capital, with which to enable it to attempt the same adventure elsewhere.

It is to be remembered that all accounts agree that the region of Kansas is the most desirable part of America now open to the emigrant. It is accessible in seven days continuous travel from Boston. Its crops are very bountiful,—its soil being well adapted to the staples of Virginia and Kentucky, and especially to the growth of hemp. In its eastern section the woodland and prairie-land intermix in proportions, very well adapted for the purposes of the settler. Its mineral resources, especially its coal, in the central and Western parts, are inexhaustible. A steamboat is already plying on the Kansas river, and the Territory has uninterrupted steamboat communication with New Orleans, and all the tributaries of the Mississippi river. All the overland emigration to California and Oregon, by any of the easier routes, passes of necessity through its limits. Whatever roads are built westward must begin in its Territory. For it is here that the emigrant leaves the Missouri river. Of late years the demand for provisions and breadstuffs made by emigrants proceeding to California, has given to the inhabitants of the neighboring parts of Missouri a market, at as good rates as they could have found in the Union.

It is impossible that such a region should not fill up rapidly. The Emigrant Aid Company proposes to give confidence to settlers, by giving system to emigration. By dispelling the fears that Kansas will be a slave State,—the Company will remove the only bar which now hinders its occupation by free settlers. It is to be hoped that similar companies will be formed in other free States. The enterprise is of that character, that for those who first enter it, the more competition the better.

It is recommended that the first settlement made by the Trustees, shall receive the name of that city in this Commonwealth which shall have subscribed most liberally to the capital stock of the Company, in proportion to its last decennial valuation; and that the second settlement be named from the city next in order so subscribing.

II. RESOURCES OF KANSAS.

The Secretary is constantly receiving Letters from various sections of the Country, asking for information respecting the Kansas Territory; such as, what may be the nature of the soil, the temperature of the region, the facilities of access to it, the navigableness of its streams, the state of the seasons as compared with our own, the means of procuring provisions, agricultural implements, &c.

The Emigrant Company has now several agents in Kansas, ascertaining its resources, both mineral and agricultural, for the purpose of aiding in making judicious selections of localities for settlement. This information and all other of general interest relating to this Territory, will, from time to time, be made public.

In the mean while, at the request of the Trustees, the Secretary has selected, from the correspondence on file, several articles of general interest. The first of these, "Notes," &c., was received from its author, Mr. Park,* who made a trip up the Kansas river, in June last, for the express purpose of acquiring, by personal observation and careful research, that definite information, so all important for the immigrant to possess. A correspondent states that Mr. P. "has had long experience on the frontier, and in the course of his narrative gives his observations on the soil, and his notices of the timbered portion of

* The senior editor of the Industrial Luminary, a weekly paper, published at $2 per annum, in advance, at Parkville, Platte Co., Missouri. Mr. P. promises to communicate further with the public, through the medium of this paper, and to furnish intelligence on a great variety of topics, which will be interesting to those who contemplate removing to the Territory referred to.

the country, and the spots best adapted for locations, town sites, &c."

Upon a careful perusal of the "Notes," and a comparison thereof, with other materièl which has appeared, they are found fraught with information, such as is now eagerly sought after, much greater in amount, more graphically communicated, and condensed in less space than can readily be found elsewhere; it is therefore thought no better service can be done to the thousands whose attention is now directed Kansas-wise, than by causing them to be issued in a convenient pamphlet form.

"NOTES OF A TRIP UP KANSAS RIVER, INCLUDING OBSERVATIONS ON THE SOIL, CLIMATE, SCENERY, &c.

BY GEO. S. PARK.

In compliance with an invitation from Capt. Baker and C. A. Perry, Esq., the enterprising owners of the fine little steamer 'Excel,' we stepped on board at Parkville, on Friday, 16th June, as one of the pleasure party up the Kansas and Smoky Hill Rivers. And here let us say that too much praise cannot be awarded to these gentlemen for the successful efforts they have made and are still making, to find the channel and establish the navigation of the Kansas River; they have already accomplished some half dozen successive trips to Fort Riley; have delivered there all necessary government freight, with a speed, care, and a saving of expense, hitherto unknown; and they have further concluded to keep their fleet little craft on that river, for the purpose of aiding settlers in reaching, with comfort and convenience, the places of their destination in the beautiful Kansas country, so long as the stage of water will admit. This resolve of theirs is good, and will be at once profitable as a business arrangement, and well-timed as an immense convenience to immigrants. We do cordially wish them, as the pioneers of steamboat navigation in this gem of the far-west,—KANSAS,—all the honor, and all the profit to which their industry and enterprise so richly entitle them.

Our party was a most agreeable one; consisting of Dr. Hammond, U. S. A., and lady—Miss Nisbet of Philadelphia, sister of Mrs. Hammond—Mrs. Perry and Mrs. Baker, with their families—Mr. Mills, Paymaster's Clerk,—Mr. Castleman of Delaware—Mr. Murdoch of New York—Mr. McCann of Virginia—and our gentlemanly officers, Messrs. Baker, Perry, and Dixon. The excursionists were not numerous; there were, however, enough to constitute an agreeable and pleasant company. The ladies of our party were the first who have sailed up this beautiful river of the Prairies.

Casting loose from the landing at Parkville, we passed rapidly down to Kansas City; and, late the same evening, leaving the eddying waters of the 'Mad Missouri,' turning her prow towards the setting sun, heading gaily towards the Rocky mountains, the 'Excel' was steaming at a fine rate up the Kansas. It is more than 600 yards wide at the mouth. The water of this river is mixed with a sandy sediment, like the Missouri; but it is freer from snags, the banks are less liable to wash and fall in, and the current is not nearly so rapid. For the first hundred miles or so, its average width will reach 600 yards; from Pattawatomie to Big Blue, 400 yards; from Big Blue to Fort Riley, 200 yards. The Pawnee or Republican, and Smoky Hill forks, are scarcely 100 yards wide. The Smoky Hill is the narrowest and deepest. Below Uniontown (about one hundred and thirty miles, by water, from the Missouri River,) the Kansas is quite straight, but above that point, it is crooked. It will be a good navigable river for two or three months in each year—perhaps for three or four in wet seasons; penetrating westward, as it does, into the heart of the Continent, it therefore must become most important in a commercial point of view.

Some of our company joined us at Delaware. Above that place the land is heavily timbered on both sides of the river—with some wide, high bottoms on either bank, consisting of high, dry, rich alluvion. Every five or six miles in this region we passed fine bluffs on the river; and on our right, immediately below the mouth of 'Stranger,' there is a beautiful one, with open woods, and high, rolling prairie in the background. Just above the junction of that stream with the Kansas River, there is a great bend, like a horse-shoe, where a tract of excellent, high bottom land can be easily inclosed by a short fence across the neck. On the south side of the river, opposite that bend, there is a pretty town site, rising gradually back from the edge of the water—the plat covered with grass and scattering timber, forming a green lawn backed with high prairies. In this neighborhood the shore is rocky. We passed a bald bluff on the north, with a rich bottom on the south side, and a high, open lawn in the rear. A little farther on, the elevated prairies strike the river, giving a charming variety to the scenery—while on the north are extended bottoms of rich timbered land.

In this vicinity we saw many Indians along the banks; we also passed a grape thicket, in the bottom, spread over several thousands of acres—while just above, on our right, rose a rocky bluff, covered with open woods. A little way above this, Sugar Creek empties into the Kansas, from the right; and a little farther up, there is a low bluff—a short distance beyond, there being another fine grape thicket, and rich walnut bottom. On the right side of the river coal has been found; and here, again, rises a beautiful undulating eminence, affording a magnificent site for a town, on the height there being open woods, and a fine prairie about a mile back.

On the left, a short distance above, the Wakarusa flows in—a considerable stream, with good timber for some way back. Below the mouth there is a good bluff, and behind are the Wakarusa settlements. Here the Methodist Church (North) have a mission. Coal has also been discovered above the Wakarusa. The Shawnees have sold, without reserve, all their lands in this direction; and the whole country on the south side of the Kansas, *above*, on its waters (except a strip five miles wide, and thirty miles long, owned by the Pattawatomies,) is now open to settlement. There will probably be some vacant lands *below*, after the Shawnees have made their selections.

In this connection it may properly be remarked, that the Wyandots own thirty-nine sections in the forks of the Kansas and Missouri rivers. The Delawares, by their recent treaty, reserve a strip ten miles wide and forty miles long, running up nearly to the mouth of the Grasshopper. The Kansas Indians, too, have a reservation twenty-two miles long, by one mile wide, north of the river, below Pattawatomie; while the Pattawatomies have thirty miles square, partly on each side of the Kansas—and the Kickapoos hold a small reserve near the head of Grasshopper. All the balance of the vast regions, drained by the Kansas river and its tributaries are now open for settlement, and will soon arrest the attention of the enterprising settlers.

On both sides of the river, above the Wakarusa, there are excellent bottom lands; and, a short way beyond these, another fine site for a town presents itself on the north side—while still farther up on the south bank, the high prairie comes right down to the water's edge, presenting another appropriate place, where the busy hum of commerce may by and by speak the presence of a city. Here we saw numerous cabins of settlers; and away, as far as the eye could reach, in a southwesterly direction, the prairies were high and rolling like the waves of Old Ocean. Southward, beautiful groves dot the prairie, and the dark line of timber that stretches along the Wakarusa valley—with the great Prairie-mound, so to speak, fixed there as the land mark of perpetual beauty—the meandering river, with its dark skirting forests of timber on the north—all are scenes in Nature's magnificent Panorama, here brought within range of vision. Proceeding north, high rich bottoms extend for many miles, and we saw vast thickets of grape-vines, pea-vines, raspberries, and pawpaws. The timber was principally oak, walnut, ash, hickory, mulberry, hackberry, linden, cottonwood, and coffee-bean.

A few miles below the mouth of the Grasshopper, on the north, the prairie undulates gradually back from the river as far as the eye can reach. At its confluence with the Kansas, there is on the opposite shore, a beautiful bluff; and between the Grasshopper and Mud Creek, there is a prairie bottom where pioneers were making claims. Capt. Baker thinks that from this point to the mouth of the Kansas is a distance of 80 miles by the river.

For the next twenty miles the country in our course presented the same general features as those just given—on both sides, alternating prairie and timber, all capable of settlement. We passed Mr. Stinson's ferry; his house and farm are very picturesquely situated on an eminence where the upland and prairies come down to the river.

About one hundred miles from the mouth of Kansas (by Capt. Baker's estimate) we passed, on the north side, a fine bluff with clumps of trees on the top, rich rolling prairie in the background, and heavy timber above and below. A little farther up, on the left bank, a high prairie bottom comes in, which swells gracefully away southward, with copes of timber, presenting to the enraptured pioneer sites for the choicest farms. Settlements are being made there on both sides of the river.

Passing onward, we come to the mouth of Soldier Creek, which has its rise far up north, and gives variety to the landscape by its dark line of fringing timber. We next saw Pappan's Ferry. His house is on the right, in a fine timbered bottom; while on the south, high prairies, such as we have already noticed, come down to the river. Here we crossed the

Pattawatomie line, about one hundred and fifteen miles from the mouth of the Kansas. Timber, on both sides of the river, were next passed—the prairie bluffs, on the south, about one hundred feet high—soon after which, we reached the Great Crossing. There are three ferries together—with Pattawatomie settlements, stores, and the Baptist School and Mission on the south side; and, every few miles beyond, there was the same succession of groves and prairie on either hand, presenting unequalled situations for farms.

Uniontown was next seen. It is made up of about twenty log cabins, and is situated on the south bank, about a mile from the river. Steaming onward, we passed Red Bluffs and Darling's Ferry; and a little farther beyond is Mill Creek, a considerable stream, on which the Pattawatomies have erected a mill. The soil here is of a red mulatto color, and is very productive; up this little river we saw fine groves of timber, and many high mounds, forming scenery of surpassing beauty.

Above Mill Creek, on the south, we passed an excellent prairie town site. A little farther, on the same side, there are lofty banks of red marl, with high prairie in the rear. We saw a large band of Indians who had been holding a council in the neighborhood, and here the carcase of a huge buffalo floated past. Again we had the rich bottoms and prairies on either side of us; and when we could withdraw our gaze from the country near by, we caught glimpses of the splendid portions stretching away far beyond. Coming to an Indian wood yard, fifteen cords of wood were taken on board, for which was paid the sum of $37,50. This is a new employment, as well as a profitable one for the red men; and the owners promised to have fifteen or twenty cords more ready by the time the steamer returned. Our fine little craft was a most interesting sight to most of them; and she was examined from the bank by over a hundred, whom curiosity had drawn together to see what had made such a shrill whistle! They were very animated; and commerce may yet infuse industrious habits into many of the Indian race.

About a mile farther up, and a little back from the river, is the Catholic Mission. Skimming along for about twenty-five miles farther, we reached the mouth of Vermillion River, emptying from the north, the timber on its banks forming a dark line through the landscape for many miles along its course. Two miles or so, above, we passed the western Pattawatomie line—supposed to be about one hundred and seventy miles, by water, from the mouth of the river.

And from this western line, let it be remarked, all the country westward and northward is open for settlement.

From this boundary to its mouth, the Kansas River presses on the southern bank, touching the uplands every four or five miles; while on the north side, from a point just below the mouth of the Blue, down some fifty miles, there is a continuous bottom, four or five miles wide—larger and more magnificent than the far-famed American Bottoms, below St. Louis. Here excellent corn has been raised by the half breeds for many years. The soil is a black, sandy loam—kind, warm, and quick; and produces much earlier in the season than farms in the same latitude east. Emigrants to California and Oregon, who are aware of this fact, prefer to cross the Missouri River, at Parkville, and take the great road up the Kansas Valley, on the north side, on this account. They find most excellent grazing for their stock by the 1st of April, often earlier. We have not seen a swamp or wet slough, nor any stagnant water, in the valley drained by the Kansas River. The streams, generally speaking, flow over gravelly beds; most of the bottoms are high; the few that are low are of a dry, sandy character; and the prairies are rolling enough to drain off the water freely.

Passing the west line of the Pattawatomie nation, we entered upon open prairie, often reaching the river on both sides; now and then a small grove, and a light fringe of timber on the banks. On the right, in a great prairie bottom, in a bend of the river extending back to Rock Creek, Mr. Perry has made a selection for a stock farm; and a little way above his claim there is another great bend, offering a tempting inducement to some other enterprising farmer who has a taste for stock raising. Beyond this we passed a large grove of timber on the right, and then passed a most appropriate bluff for a town site—the first we saw for several miles. Here we saw Blue Hill, which is a prominent landmark overlooking the mouth of Blue river. From this point upward, the bluffs are higher and more abrupt, and the country back more elevated and broken. Here we saw a large eagle nest, out of which the old bird looked angrily at us, for intruding on its pre-emption; but she, too, must give way, with the red skins, to manifest destiny. A little way above, another huge buffalo floated past; he may have been anxious to slake his thirst in the Republican or Smokyhill, lost foothold, and got carried away by the rolling flood.

Passing the mouth of the Blue, which comes in from the north, (as nearly all the tributaries of Kansas do,) and appears to be navigable for some distance, we were pleased with its fine bottoms and long streak of timber; while on the left, were conical bluffs and high prairie mounds, with figured lines, and steps rising one above another in the distance, contributing to the scenery a very romantic appearance. Immediately above this important tributary, there is another beautiful prairie bottom, sloping back northward farther than we could see; and on the left, still another, containing more than 2000 acres, in a bend not more than three-fourths of a mile across the neck.—The enticing features of the latter are—a little grove of timber on the height, a cool gushing spring, and plenty of rock at hand in the bluff, with which to raise an enduring fence over the narrow isthmus. The world does not present a more excellent situation for a stock farm; indeed, the whole line of the main river and branches, from here upward, may be said to be adapted for a continuous series of such farms. On the right a bluff comes into the river, the first above the mouth of the Blue, offering an appropriate town site; and we saw stakes set on the slope, as well as a tent or cabin back on the high prairie—indicating that our countrymen were there. Just above, there is a clear, running stream, and a line of timber reaching far back. From this to the Fort, the river winds like a natural canal, through green flowery meadows, with similar scenery in the distance. On the left, we saw some splendid country for farms, up the valley of a stream, the name of which we do not recollect; there were fine groves of timber, and rich valley land. We understand that several claims have been made there.

On Monday night, just before reaching Fort Riley, we were overtaken by a tremendous thunder storm. We were surrounded by prairie; and the captain had to lay his craft close to the shore, and cast anchor, there being no stump or tree to hitch to. He is of opinion, that there should not be a cabin on steamers navigating these prairie rivers, where the winds sometimes sweep along with unbroken violence. We saw the Pilot Mounds in the distance, where the military road leaves the Kansas bottoms, and passes through a depression in the bluff to the crossing of the Blue. We passed some small creeks on the right, with settlements on them; and Clark's Creek, on the left, affording some fine timbered lands, and good springs.

A little after sunrise, on Tuesday morning, we neared Fort Riley—its fine stone buildings looming up grandly in the sunbeams. It is located at the junction of the Republican and Smokyhill forks of the Kansas, on the second bench or roll of the prairie, having higher bluffs immediately behind, from which the building rock is quarried. It is soft limestone, easily cut into with a pick, and can be split into any shape; we noticed the same horizontal strata cropping out at all elevated points in the prairie. Crossing the Pawnee or Republican fork by the Government bridge, we had a good view of the fine country between the two rivers, which rises gracefully backward in high, swelling prairies. Here there is a saw mill just started. We strolled up the Republican, gathered some black raspberries, and crossed a spring branch, then mounted a high bluff, whence we could see the beautiful Republican Valley a long way up. It is nearly three miles wide, high, dry, and level, with a loose, black, rich soil. The river flows in a serpentine course through the prairie bottoms, at some bends making nearly a circuit of six or eight miles, and coming back to within a mile of itself again—the banks generally having a light fringe of timber, with occasional groves near the water's edge, in the ravines, and on the bluffs. This is truly a delightful valley—the most inviting for settlement we ever saw.

The 'Excel' made a short trip up Smokyhill, Lieut. Sargent, from the Fort, accompanied us. We had an exciting time. The constant announcement from the man who heaved the lead, was, 'No bottom.' The river was full, and the current strong, but we had great difficulty in getting round the short bends;—it keeps on the course of the main Kansas, coming a little more from the south-west. There is more timber on this river than on the Kansas above Pattawatomie, and the soil is better. We observed a deep marl deposit on the bluffs, beneath black soil, and the bottoms inclined up prettily from the river. A little way up, we saw a band of Fox Indians crossing over, going north on a buffalo-hunt; and their motley procession stretched along over the prairies for miles. Here and there in the party was carried a pole, with a swan's neck or eagle's head and tail, &c., stuck upon it for a flag. They had with them about five hundred horses, all of which looked well. Great was the surprise manifested on seeing the 'Excel' puffing along up these unknown waters; but, poor fellows! the startling scream of the shrill steam whistle, and the impetuous snorting of the iron-horse, will soon scare off the buffalo and other game from your hunting-grounds, to return no more—you too must follow in their trail, or succumb to the irresistible influence of civilization.

Some forty miles up Smokyhill, an extensive bed of gypsum has been found, specimens of which have been tested and proved to be of superior quality; we brought a small specimen home with us. Salt is also alleged to be very abundant on the Saline fork; the waters of the Smokyhill are often quite brackish, and when the boilers of the 'Excel' are filled from that river, there is a slight incrustation of salt deposited. Specimens of coal, both bituminous and anthracite, and of tin, lead, and iron ore, have been brought in. Hints have been given that gold abounds, but in parts—*unknown!* There cannot be a doubt, however, that valuable minerals will be found cropping out beneath, or interspersed in the primitive formation, as we ascend toward the Rocky Mountains. The country rises very rapidly in that direction from Fort Riley; up the Republican, for instance, the ascent, in the first three hundred miles, is said to be two thousand feet. The rock in vicinity of Smokyhill is principally limestone; and the river bottoms are a sandy loam. The upland prairies are broken, but of black, rich soil, particularly where limestone predominates; the valleys are also very rich, and the soil mellow. Passing over the high uplands, often there is nothing to be seen but prairie spreading out beyond, till it is lost in dim distance; when all at once, as if by magic, you come upon a

'Woody valley, warm and low,'—

with fine springs and clear running water. This is, indeed, a well-watered region, and must be salubrious and healthy. We previously mentioned the scarcity of timber above Pattawatomie; it may here be added, that it is inadequate to supply what would be needed for agricultural purposes, and hardly sufficient for firewood. Here and to the westward, a new era in agriculture must be inaugurated—a new system must be practised. Nature demands that it should be so. Instead of clearing timber lands, as in Eastern States, the citizen-farmers of Kansas must grow their timber. There is fuel wanted, but coal, in many places, can be got with little labor; houses must be built, and fences made, but in the absence of sufficient timber, excellent rock for all purposes can be procured in abundance; or, for fencing, the farmer can hedge himself in most completely with Osage Orange. The country abounds with the most luscious grapes. Stock of all kinds are remarkably healthy; and these rolling prairies will make the finest sheep-walks in the world. In fact, this may be designated the PASTORAL REGION OF AMERICA. The gardens at Fort Riley look well; and we procured some beautiful wild prairie flowers.

The difficulty of navigating the Smokyhill with a stern-wheel steamer of such length as the 'Excel,' prevented Capt. Baker from venturing so far up as he otherwise would. A shorter side-wheel steamer, of very light draught, adapted to the navigation of these interior rivers, will soon be put on the trade. We left Fort Riley on the return trip, on Wednesday morning, and came down 'kiteing.' Passing rapidly in review the splendid scenery of which we have attempted to make hasty memoranda, we entered the Missouri about daylight next morning.

Before concluding these brief notes, it must be remarked—in reference to the productions and climate of Kansas Territory—that there are, no doubt, superior hemp lands in its central and western portions; but Nature unmistakably indicates stock-raising as the proper and most profitable occupation for the farmers who shall settle there. In the great Kansas Valley below Pattawatomie, and in the eastern region along the Missouri, there are some of the finest hemp lands in the world. Wheat, corn, oats, and vegetables, grow as well there as in any of the Western States. Those in the Platte Purchase, immediately east of the Missouri River, who attend to fruit-growing, say that their apples, peaches, plums, &c., cannot be surpassed anywhere; we can see no reason why as much may not be said of the same crops in the region across the river.

The winters are generally dry and pleasant, and the roads fine; but little snow falls, and this lays on the ground only for a short time. Sometimes, however, there are very 'cold spells' of weather, but they are not of long duration. For instance, the masons in Parkville, Platte Co., Mo., quarried and laid stone last winter with but little interruption on account of the weather. Common cattle, colts, mules, and sheep, can be wintered on blue-grass, provided the pastures are allowed to grow up in the Fall, and the stock have a little corn or hay occasionally. February and March are frequently quite pleasant, and much plowing can be done in the mellow dry loam of the Kansas Valley. The summers are quite warm and long, the thermometer (Fahr.) not unfrequently marking up to near one hundred degrees in the shade. The high prairies, however, are generally fanned by cool refreshing breezes; and as we ascend the branches of the Kansas from Fort Riley, there is a rapid rise to a cooler region. In May and June there is a superabundance of rain; but the latter end of summer and fall are generally dry.

Having been across the Territory many times in course of the last fifteen years, we give these remarks as the result of our experience."

In regard to the *productiveness* of the soil, and the most favorable time for immigrating to Kansas, attention is directed to the following Letter, written by a gentleman well known to the Secretary, and upon whose opinion reliance may be placed.

INDEPENDENCE, MO. JULY 17, 1854.

Dear Sir,—In my wanderings to and fro in this region, I find myself, to night, in this pleasant town, where are some fine buildings, good land, and enterprising citizens.

The Court house, situated in the centre of the square that occupies the centre of the village, is truly an elegant building. There are also at least two large and well kept hotels, as well as a great number of stores, good dwelling houses, &c., in the town. The land, like that in Kansas Territory, is rolling, rich and beautiful, and yields immense crops of corn, hemp, tobacco, and of almost any thing else that can be raised in the United States. I have passed cornfields, to-day, where some of the corn was so tall that the tallest man sitting on the tallest horse in Massachusetts would be unable to reach the top, and that, too, when it has just commenced to tassel out, and before the stalk has completed its growth. I am told that when the corn is harvested, only the tallest of the laborers can reach some of the corn without breaking down the stalks. Judging from the present appearance of the corn here, and of that in Illinois, when I passed through that State, the yield of this will be nearly or quite twice as much as that. In fact, I never saw any thing like the corn here, nor "dreamed of it in my philosophy." A very intelligent and systematic Belgian farmer, in Kansas, a few days since, gave me some of his experience in farming, with hired slaves for his laborers. According to his experience, last year, which was not so good as some, on account of the dry weather, he will have this Fall, when his harvesting is done, as follows:

Corn, eighty-five acres, with sixty-five bushels to the acre, at 50 cts. a bushel, amounting to $2,762
Wheat 10 acres, 20 bushels to the acre, at $1,00, making 200
Oats, 26 acres, 40 " " " 30, " 312
Timothy grass, 12 acres, 2 tons to the acre 10,00, " 240
Clover, 2½ acres for the swine.
Potatoes, 1 acre, 200 bushels, at 40c., making 80

These products amount to $3,594. In addition to this he has 150 swine, which, when ready for the knife, will weigh 230 lbs. each, if as good as last year, and which at six cents a pound, will come to $2,070. Deducting 18 bushels of corn at 50 cents a bushel for each hog, will leave $720; which, added to the first, makes $4,314. The work on his farm, including the garden, general improvements, &c., is done by five men, or hired slaves, while the owner simply superintends it.

From ten to fifteen hundred pounds of hemp to the acre is an average crop for this land, and the price the year past has been from 120 to 150 dollars a ton. Pumpkins, melons, apples, peaches, and fruit of all kinds, grow here in abundance if planted. Such is the land in Kansas town, and such, also, is the land in Kansas Territory; for it is of the same general character. Let it be remembered that such crops as the above are raised without a spoonful of manure, and that, too, from year to year for all time to come, for aught I know. I have seen corn growing on land that has been planted for twenty years in succession, and there was no apparent difference between it, and the corn on new land. Also, let the New England farmer remember, that to raise from 60 to 80 bushels of corn to the acre here, no *hoeing* is required. The only work requisite after planting is to plow amongst it a few times, and such work as "weeding," "half hilling," and "hilling" is unknown. The price of this land is, for unimproved, from 25 to 40 dollars an acre; and for improved land, from 40 to 100 dollars. This is the price of all the land bordering on the Territory for several miles south of the mouth of the Kansas river, and it will soon be higher—for there is comparatively but little such land in the United States as this. The land all through the Kansas river valley, in the Territory, is equally as good as that above described, and worth as much to the acre, and will produce as large crops. Is it to be wondered at, then, that every young man in Missouri, and every old man, also, who has not already a farm of the same quality of his own, should be rushing into the Territory to secure 160 acres, for $1,25 an acre, when he knows it will be worth from $25 to $100 the moment he gets his title? Rather is it not strange, and wonderful that, at least, one hundred thousand persons from New England, are not on their way to this garden of the world, at this moment? That such would be the case I have no doubt, if the good qualities of the land, climate, &c., were understood by them as well as they are by those in Missouri on the borders. The rush from this State to Kansas Territory, is *not so much to secure a foothold for slavery there,* as to secure a *fortune,* notwithstanding what the newspapers say about it. No; most who go from here are young men, in want of farms; and slavery, to say the least, is a secondary matter with them, if indeed, they are not opposed to its introduction into Kansas, which is certainly the case with many.

You ask, when is the best time for New England men to go to Kansas? Unquestionably the best time is this Fall. By coming now, they can select from the best of the land now open to settlement, as well as get their cabins and fences made, and their land plowed ready for Spring work. The winters, I am told, are so mild, that out door work can be done with comfort, such as splitting rails, fencing, building houses, &c., during most of the season. Besides, if they would be represented in the first Territorial Legislature of Kansas, they must be on the ground soon.

At some other time, I will speak of the inducements for mechanics to settle in Kansas and western Missouri. * *

As much interest is manifested in respect to the Pioneer Party, which left Boston, July 17th, a Letter from one of the number, communicated to the Boston Journal, is subjoined.

THE NEW ENGLAND EMIGRATION TO KANSAS.

St. Louis, Steamer "Polar Star."
July 24, 1854.

Mr. Editor:—Our Pioneer Party to Kansas have reached this point on their journey from Boston to the American 'Central Flowery Land.' Although the weather has been unusually warm, the journey has been pleasant, and every man is in the enjoyment of excellent health. All look forward with good spirits to their entrance upon the new homes beyond the Missouri. The company consists of thirty men, all of whom are men of intelligence and discreetness, and some of cultivation, and even of considerable property. The railroad agents, hotel keepers, and others in the western cities, who had been partially led to expect, from the ridiculous reports set afloat in pro slavery journals of the South, a flood of paupers, foreign and domestic, collected from the streets of Northern cities, were astonished. They counted not upon seeing a body of sober and substantial citizens, embracing, besides men of the four Professions of theology, law, medicine and teaching, several enterprising master manufacturers and mechanics and sturdy farmers. From the character of the present party of emigrants, the Country may expect soon to see in Kansas a flourishing community, based on the old upright New England principles, and the wealth of several of them, and of those connected in business with them at home, will enable them quickly to put up saw mills and other manufactories. Such in fact is the intention.

No where has the Party been more kindly received than in St. Louis. We are visited daily by intelligent citizens, who express a warm interest in the movement. We are assured that throughout the State the great bulk of the honest inhabitants desire just such a neighbor State as an encouraged emigration from the respectable inhabitants of the North would make of Kansas. The Jackson and Platte County resolutions are denounced in the strongest terms, and you will see that already the back track is taken, and that some of the papers in that section of the State are endeavoring to put a very harmless construction upon them, and one altogether different from the obvious meaning. We are told that at another meeting, held in one of the border counties quite recently, similar resolutions against Northern emigration were voted down, eight to one. We apprehend no trouble. Popular sentiment has been too decidedly manifested against the fanaticism of the late Jackson County meeting. However, come what may, our thirty New Englanders are not likely to be terrified by bravado, and whilst they disclaim any interference with Missouri slaveholders, will not be imposed upon themselves.

It is right to say that the party feel entirely satisfied with the operations of the Emigrant Aid Company. A meeting was held at the City Hotel, in St. Louis, on Saturday evening, of which Hugh Cameron, of Washington, D. C. was Chairman, and Edwin Davenport, of Boston, Secretary. After making a thorough organization of themselves for effectual co-operation and protection, a series of resolutions expressive of the high confidence entertained in the Massachusetts Emigrant Aid Society was passed. They were forwarded to the officers of that Society, and will be published by them if they think fit.

We start in the "Polar Star," tomorrow evening, and will disembark at the mouth of the Kansas River. There we shall meet with the Company's guides. I will write you again.

After an exceedingly hot day, it is now (4 o'clock) raining heavily, accompanied with very heavy thunder.

Charlestown.

www.ingramcontent.com/pod-product-compliance
Lightning Source LLC
LaVergne TN
LVHW020634110826
845149LV00004B/1175